MASTERING THE BOULDERING

Comprehensive Guide to Bouldering Techniques, Climbing Tips, Training Workouts, Safety, Gear, Grades, Routes, and Skills for Beginners and Enthusiasts

THOMPSONE T. CASTILLO

COPYRIGHT © 2023 BY THOMPSONE T. CASTILLO

All rights reserved. No part of this publication may be reproduced, distributed, or transmitted in any form or by any means, including photocopying, recording, or other electronic or mechanical methods, without the prior written permission of the publisher, except in the case of brief quotations embodied in critical reviews and certain other noncommercial uses permitted by copyright law.

CHAPTER ONE 5

GETTING STARTED WITH BOULDERING 5

Bouldering vs. Climbing: Important Distinctions 9

Equipment and Gear for Bouldering 11

CHAPTER TWO 17

LEARNING THE BASICS OF BOULDERING 17

Selecting the Best Bouldering Shoes 18

Picking Out Chalk and Chalk Bags 21

Crash Pads: Use and Importance 22

OUTDOOR VS. INDOOR BOULDERING 27

Bouldering Indoors 27

Bouldering outdoors: 28

CHAPTER THREE 31

BASIC BOULDERING TECHNIQUES 31

Correct Body Position for Bouldering 32

Footwork and Accurate Foot Position ... 37

CHAPTER FOUR 44

BOULDERING TRAINING AND SAFETY.........44

Finger Power and Injury Avoidance 51

Training for the Open-Hand Grip: 52

Training Exercises for Bouldering..........54

CHAPTER FIVE 58

BOULDERING PROGRESSION AND CHALLENGES...58

Setting Goals for Bouldering and Monitoring Progress..............................59

Understanding Bouldering Routes and Problems 61

Working Through Cruxes and Sequences in Technical Issues...................................63

Techniques for Solving Issues and Beta 65

Physical and mental rest: 68

CHAPTER SIX 71

BOULDERING OUTSIDE AND BEYOND 71

Morality and the Leave No Trace Guidelines 74

Adapting to the Challenges of Outdoor Climbing 78

Bouldering as a Lifestyle: Connection and Exploration 80

THANK YOU 84

CHAPTER ONE
GETTING STARTED WITH BOULDERING

Bouldering is a dynamic and thrilling activity that has been more popular in recent years due to its distinctive combination of physical difficulty and mental involvement. Bouldering, which has its roots in rock climbing, is a style of climbing that emphasizes shorter routes, or "problems," without the use of ropes or harnesses. Climbers must negotiate complex patterns of grips on rocks or indoor climbing walls in this strenuous and skill-demanding pastime. The specifics of bouldering will be covered in this introduction, including its definition, advantages for strength and agility, how it differs from regular climbing, the gear and equipment needed, and the intricate system of bouldering grades and ratings.

Bouldering's fundamental activity is climbing short, difficult routes that call on a combination of strength, balance, technique, and problem-solving skills. Boulderers, sometimes known as climbers, navigate around made-up or unmade surfaces that resemble natural rock formations. Bouldering difficulties can range in difficulty, providing routes suitable for both inexperienced and experienced climbers. Bouldering is frequently done indoors on climbing walls with padding for safety, but aficionados also like doing it outdoors on real rock formations.

Strength and agility advantages of bouldering

Bouldering is a thorough workout that has many positive effects on the body and the mind. Its capacity to improve both strength and agility is one of its main advantages. While bouldering, different muscle groups are constantly used, which encourages the growth of muscles and increases overall body strength. For complex grips and difficult motions, climbers use their grip strength, core, upper body, and lower body. The emphasis on body alignment and balance helps to develop agility and coordination as well as strength.

Bouldering also offers a cardiovascular exercise because climbers use dynamic movements and keep their heart rates raised throughout their sessions. Bouldering is a quick and efficient form of training since it combines strength and cardio.

Bouldering vs. Climbing: Important Distinctions

Although bouldering and climbing are comparable, they are two different sports that fall under the umbrella of rock-based activities. Bouldering focuses on quick, challenging routes that might be as short as a few moves and as tall as 20 feet. Climbers navigate these issues by using a lot of technique, power, and precision.

On the other hand, traditional climbing includes longer routes and frequently calls for the use of ropes, harnesses, and other safety gear. As climbers may spend considerable time scaling multi-pitch routes that can take hours or even days to accomplish, this style of climbing emphasizes endurance.

Equipment and Gear for Bouldering

When it comes to equipment and gear, bouldering is known for its simplicity. Climbing is a sport that is accessible to novices because it requires minimum equipment. Crash pads, chalk, and climbing shoes are among the necessary accessories.

In order to navigate grips successfully, climbing shoes offer the essential grip and dexterity. Climbers can make precise movements with the help of these shoes' snug fit and unique rubber bottoms that are made to grab holds.

The climbers' hands are kept dry and their grip is improved by the use of chalk, which is typically in the form of loose powder or a chalk ball. This is crucial because perspiration can diminish friction in the hands, which can impair performance.

Crash pads are a crucial part of bouldering's safety setup, especially when climbing outside. To cushion falls and reduce the chance of harm, these sizable foam pads are positioned at the base of the boulder.

Comprehending Bouldering Ratings and Grades

Bouldering issues are given grades and ratings to let climbers know how challenging they are. Due to their complexity and diversity across various grading systems, these grades can first be difficult to understand.

One of the most popular bouldering grading systems, particularly in the United States, is the V-scale. The greater the number, the harder the task is, according to this approach, which was created by John Sherman and uses a numerical system followed by the letter "V." The type of holds, the complexity of the moves, and the level of difficulty of the route all affect the grade.

The Fontainebleau system, sometimes known as the "Font" system, is well-liked in Europe. The more complex grading scale used in this method contains both letters and numbers, with higher numbers and letters denoting harder work. The technical and physical difficulties of the climb are heavily stressed in the Fontainebleau system.

For climbers to choose challenges that match their skill level and increasingly challenge themselves as they advance, an understanding of various grading systems is crucial. Climbers may, however, see variations in difficulty ratings between various climbing gyms and outdoor bouldering locales due to the subjective nature of grading.

Bouldering is an engaging activity with a variety of facets that combines physical effort with cerebral challenge. It is a distinctive exercise that attracts those looking for a hard yet fulfilling experience due to its emphasis on strength, agility, technique, and problem-solving. As bouldering continues to increase in popularity, it exposes fans to a lively community and a welcoming setting for introspection and discovery. Bouldering is a sport that may be performed either indoors on manufactured walls or outdoors on real rock formations, and it is a monument to the boundless potential of human physical and mental ability.

CHAPTER TWO
LEARNING THE BASICS OF BOULDERING

With its unique combination of physical difficulty and mental involvement, bouldering presents a fascinating entry point into the world of climbing. It's essential to arm yourself with the tools and information you'll need before setting out on your adventure in order to guarantee a secure and happy experience. This manual will walk you through all of the necessary procedures for beginning bouldering, including selecting the appropriate footwear, comprehending bouldering holds, and deciding whether to boulder indoors or outdoors.

Selecting the Best Bouldering Shoes

The cornerstone of your climbing equipment, bouldering shoes have a significant impact on both your performance and comfort while on the wall. You can confidently carry out complex motions thanks to the specific grip and precision these shoes are made to offer on holds. Several considerations must be made when selecting climbing footwear:

Fit:

Shoes for climbing must fit snugly. Your toes shouldn't be severely crushed when they contact the front of the shoe. Your sensitivity to the holds is increased thanks to the tight fit, which also ensures superior control.

Climbing Style:

Take into account the kind of climbing you'll be doing. Shoes having a more extreme descent (curved shape) are frequently favored for bouldering. This shape helps you tackle overhangs and difficult holds by improving the power and accuracy of your footwork.

Materials and Finish:

Shoes for bouldering come in a variety of materials and fastenings. While synthetic shoes maintain their original fit over time, leather shoes tend to expand and conform to your foot shape with time. Lace-up, Velcro, and slip-on closure methods are all available, and each has benefits for ease and adjustability.

Picking Out Chalk and Chalk Bags

A climber's best buddy is chalk since it keeps your hands dry and makes it easier to grip grips. There are two major types of chalk: loose chalk and chalk balls. Applying loose chalk involves rubbing your hands together after dipping them in a chalk bag or bucket to spread the chalk out evenly. The mess-free alternative is chalk balls, which are compacted chalk inside a mesh or fabric pouch.

Think about the texture and degree of dampness in your hands while choosing chalk. A chalk with a higher magnesium carbonate content is preferred for better drying action if you frequently have sweaty hands. Additionally, purchasing a quality chalk bag is crucial. Chalk bags are made to be conveniently accessible when climbing so that you can swiftly add chalk mid-route without losing momentum.

Crash Pads: Use and Importance

Bouldering requires extreme caution, especially when done outdoors. Large foam pads called crash pads are used to cushion falls and lessen the chance of harm during hard landings. They are an essential piece of equipment, especially when bouldering on erratic and uneven natural rock formations.

Placement is crucial when employing crash pads. Place them under the climb in carefully chosen positions, paying attention to potential fall zones. To make sure the crash cushions are placed correctly, consult your climbing partner or group. You will have a better grasp of fall trajectories and the best locations for crash pads as you advance in bouldering.

Recognizing Bouldering Grip and Holds

Bouldering holds exist in a variety of sizes and shapes, and mastering their utilization is crucial to solving challenges. Here are a few prevalent holds and grips:

Jug:

It has a big, strong grip that's simple to use with an open hand. Jugs are excellent for pausing or changing movements.

Crimp:

A little hold that necessitates bending your fingers in order to grasp it. Strong finger strength and the right technique are necessary for crimping to prevent harm.

Sloper:

A grip without positive edges that is spherical and smooth. Slopers must maintain strong balance and body tension in order to stay on the wall.

Pinch:

A grip including pinching it between your thumb and fingers. Pinch tests measure your pinch strength and frequently come in several configurations.

Pocket:

A manageable, rounded grasp that is small and compact. Different-sized pockets test your finger dexterity and accuracy.

In order to advance in bouldering, it is crucial to master various hold configurations and grips. You'll develop the ability to modify your technique to the particular qualities of each hold as you acquire experience.

OUTDOOR VS. INDOOR BOULDERING

The choice of climbing indoors versus outdoors is one that a boulderer must make. Both choices come with specific benefits and things to think about:

Bouldering Indoors

Indoor climbing gyms offer a safe environment with a wide range of grips and routes. Regardless of the weather, they are fantastic for honing your talents. Indoor climbing is a great place for beginners to start because it also provides a supportive environment and coaching options.

Bouldering outdoors:

Bouldering in a natural setting provides a sense of connection to the environment and the accomplishment of overcoming actual rock. However, it necessitates extra factors, such as safety, accessibility, and environmental impact. Outdoor bouldering involves important considerations such as learning outdoor etiquette, abiding by local laws, and leaving no trace.

Whether you go for indoor or outdoor bouldering, keep in mind that both activities will help you become a better climber. Your adventure in bouldering will be enriched by the unique rewards and challenges presented by each venue.

In summary, learning how to boulder needs more than simply physical prowess; it also necessitates careful consideration of gear selection, technique, and environment. Making the decision between indoor and outdoor climbing and selecting the proper shoes, chalk, and crash pads are all crucial first steps in the bouldering process. Remember to put safety first as you get involved in this thrilling sport, pick up tips from seasoned climbers, and take pleasure in pushing your physical and mental limits. Bouldering provides a way to increase strength and agility as well as a sense of success and a friendly community of others who share your hobby.

CHAPTER THREE
BASIC BOULDERING TECHNIQUES

A strong foundation of techniques is necessary for bouldering, a physically taxing and mentally exciting sport, to successfully negotiate the demands of various routes. Learning these skills improves your performance while lowering your chance of injury and fostering effective climbing. We'll explore the core skills that every boulderer needs to know in this book, including the appropriate body position for bouldering, a variety of handholds, accurate footwork, balance and weight shifting, and the execution of dynamic movements with synchronization.

Correct Body Position for Bouldering

The key to successful bouldering is maintaining the right body position. Your strength, balance, and control on the wall are all maximized when your body is in the right posture.

Important elements of the ideal body position include:

Core Participation:

To maintain stability and prevent overextension, contract your core muscles. You can better regulate your motions and keep a steady center of gravity by having a strong core.

Rotating the hips

Holds while positioning your hips in reference to the wall. You can more easily attain holds and produce power for dynamic techniques with proper hip rotation.

Calm Feet:

Keep your lower body, especially your feet, as still as possible. Quieter feet use less energy and improve foot placement accuracy.

Do not over-grip:

Premature exhaustion can result from overgripping or holding grips too firmly. To save energy and have a relaxed grip on grips, use only the appropriate amount of grip force.

Handholds: Slopers, Crimps, Pinches, etc.

Bouldering holds come in a variety of shapes and need specialized usage methods to be used effectively. Understanding several holds enables you to customize your strategy for any issue:

Crimps:

Small grips called crimps need dexterity and finger strength. Focus on using your fingertips rather than your palm to grasp these holds with your fingers bent.

Slopers:

Slopers are rounded, smooth grips without sharp edges. Engage your core, maintain your posture, and use open-handed grips to evenly distribute pressure as you battle slopers.

Pinches:

In order to pinch, you must pinch your thumb and fingers together. Maintain a steady grip and modify your body position to produce the best optimal angle when using pinches.

Jugs:

Jugs are easy to handle with an open hand because of their size and positive grip. When faced with jugs, concentrate on moving quickly and save your energy for the harder areas.

Footwork and Accurate Foot Position

Your climbing efficiency and balance are significantly impacted by your footwork, which is a fundamental ability. In addition to making it easier to reach holds, good foot placement also helps you evenly distribute your weight:

Calm Feet:

Reduce the force of your foot placements by softly touching grips. This saves energy and prevents you from losing your balance against the wall.

Smears and edges:

On tiny grips or edges, use the edges of your climbing shoes. When smearing, you put your foot on a volume or hold with less surface area and use friction to keep your foot there.

Hooking and Flagging

To stay balanced, flagging entails extending one leg to the side. In order to aid in stabilization or advance to the next move, hooking is the technique of using your heel or toe to catch or hook onto holds.

Balance and Weight Shifting on a Wall

To retain control and save energy when climbing, balance is a crucial component of bouldering technique:

Weight Allocation

Aim to equally distribute your weight between your hands and feet and refrain from overusing any one limb. This encourages stability and lessens the stress on particular muscle groups.

Weight Change:

To improve your grasp on holds, deliberately shift your weight. You may avoid over-gripping and maintain control during dynamic movements by shifting your weight properly.

Tense body:

Keep your muscles taut to avoid sagging or swinging. You can maintain your balance and effectiveness by using antagonistic forces between your limbs and your core.

Coordination and Dynamic Moves

Explosive movements are referred to as dynamic maneuvers and are used to reach distant holds or move between holds. Coordination, timing, and controlled power are needed for these movements:

Coordination:

To perform dynamic motions successfully, sync your hand and foot movements. Timing is very important since improper timing might lead to missed holds or ineffective motion.

Dynos:

In a dyno, both hands are taken away from the wall to grasp a grip that is farther away. Aim to maintain a regulated trajectory while producing power with your legs and core.

Holding Latches:

Aim to "latch" or firmly clutch the target hold when doing dynamic motions. To guarantee a firm grasp, work on hand-eye coordination and modify your grip when you make contact.

In conclusion, climbers of all skill levels must understand fundamental bouldering techniques. The building blocks of good bouldering are correct body alignment, knowledge of various hold types, perfect footwork, balance, and weight shifting, as well as the execution of dynamic movements with coordination. Continue to hone these methods as you go, modify them to fit various climbing circumstances, and put yourself to the test with harder issues. Keep in mind that bouldering requires more than just physical capability; you must also discover the right balance of technique, mental forethought, and physical prowess to successfully complete each route.

CHAPTER FOUR
BOULDERING TRAINING AND SAFETY

Bouldering is a thrilling sport that tests your stamina, concentration, and problem-solving abilities. But like with any athletic exercise, safety comes first. To fully enjoy bouldering while reducing the danger of harm, it is crucial to comprehend correct safety precautions and incorporate efficient training strategies. The essential elements of bouldering safety and training will be covered in this guide, including gym rules and safety precautions, falling techniques, warming up and cooling down, injury prevention, and workouts specifically designed for bouldering.

Bouldering Gym Policies and Procedures

It's important to follow certain rules and regulations while entering a bouldering gym to maintain a respectful and safe climbing environment:

Orientation and check-in:

Attend any compulsory orientation seminars and be sure to always check in at the front desk. Learn about the layout, grading, and safety protocols of the gym.

Climbing Protocol:

Allow other climbers to finish their ascents without interfering in their personal space. Share the wall politely and communicate with other climbers.

Zones of Falling:

A defined falling zone is located beneath climbing routes; be mindful of it. Crash pads are installed in these areas to reduce the possibility of injuries from falls.

Use of Equipment Properly:

Handle climbing equipment with care and in accordance with the instructions, such as ropes, carabiners, and harnesses. Before climbing, make sure to properly adjust harnesses and double-check knots.

Specific Route Safety:

Before ascending, determine how challenging the route will be. Avoid attempting a route if it is above your level of expertise to avoid undue strain and possibly harm.

Safe Falling and Landing Procedures

Bouldering inevitably involves falling, thus learning how to do so properly is crucial to avoiding injuries:

Rolling:

When you fall, practice rolling to spread the force of the impact over your body and minimize the chance of injury to particular body areas.

Tucking and Impact Absorption:

Aim to land on your feet or buttocks to distribute the force of the impact by curling yourself into a ball. When you land, bend your knees to take the impact.

Avoiding Falls with Overhangs:

To prevent swinging into the wall or other climbers when falling from an overhang, try to regulate your fall path.

Spotting:

Use spotters when climbing outside to direct your fall and make sure you land on the crash pad.

Preparing and Cooling Off

Both warming up and cooling down are essential for preventing injuries and improving performance.

Warm-Up:

Exercise light aerobically before climbing to promote blood flow to your muscles, such as jogging or jumping jacks. Exercises for joint mobility and dynamic stretches can help your body get ready for more strenuous tasks.

Taking a break:

Perform static stretches to increase flexibility and rest your muscles after your climbing workout. Concentrate on the parts of your body, such as your fingers, wrists, shoulders, and hips, that you used the most during the session.

Finger Power and Injury Avoidance

Bouldering relies heavily on finger strength, but it's important to develop it gradually to prevent overuse injuries:

Gradual Advancement:

Create moderate increases in finger strength to give your tendons and ligaments time to adjust. To prevent uncomfortable situations like pulley injuries, don't overtrain.

Training for the Open-Hand Grip:

Train with an open-hand grip, which is easier on your tendons than full crimps. The alternative grip encourages balanced finger strength.

Fingerboarding:

To isolate finger muscles for strength training, try fingerboarding. To prevent harm, it should be approached slowly and under good instruction.

Rest and Restoration

In order to avoid overuse injuries, it is crucial to get enough rest in between climbing sessions. Avoid pushing through pain by paying attention to your body.

Training Exercises for Bouldering

Bouldering-specific training drills can help you develop your climbing abilities and physical fitness:

Campus Board Education

A unique training device for developing upper body strength and dynamic movement abilities is the campus board. Use it to strengthen your grasp and perform explosive movements.

Hangboard instruction:

Hangboards are useful for developing finger strength. To prevent overexertion and injury, they should be used gradually and cautiously.

Exercises for the core and body tension

Body tension and strong core muscles are essential for preserving good body alignment. Include exercises like leg lifts, Russian twists, and planks in your routine.

Training your antagonist muscles:

To keep your muscles balanced and lower your risk of imbalances and injuries, strengthen your antagonist muscles (the muscles that are opposing to those you use for climbing).

Mobility & Flexibility at Work:

Regular mobility and flexibility workouts increase your range of motion, which is essential for executing intricate moves and reaching grips.

In order to ensure a satisfying and injury-free climbing experience, bouldering safety and training go hand in hand. Injury prevention depends on following safety laws and regulations at the gym, mastering good falling techniques, and implementing warm-up and cool-down exercises. Your total climbing prowess is influenced by your finger strength development, balanced training, and use of bouldering-specific activities. Keep in mind that safety and training are continual processes, therefore it's crucial to educate yourself frequently, pay attention to your body, and seek advice from knowledgeable climbers or trainers. The joys and challenges of bouldering may be enjoyed while putting your health and continued participation in the sport first.

CHAPTER FIVE
BOULDERING PROGRESSION AND CHALLENGES

The dynamic and ever-evolving sport of bouldering offers a constant voyage of development, self-discovery, and success. As you learn more about bouldering, you'll run into a variety of obstacles and chances to advance. This manual explores the nuances of bouldering advancement, covering everything from setting objectives and monitoring progress to deciphering routes, resolving tricky situations, using smart tactics, and overcoming plateaus.

Setting Goals for Bouldering and Monitoring Progress

Setting goals will help you grow in bouldering by providing you with motivation and direction while you attempt to advance your climbing skills:

SMART Objectives

Decide on specific, measurable, attainable, timely, relevant objectives. For instance, setting a deadline to finish a particular route grade.

Short-term and long-term objectives:

Differentiate between long-term objectives (like climbing a given grade) and short-term objectives (like perfecting a specific technique or movement).

Progress monitoring

Use a climbing notebook or a digital tool to keep track of your ascents, difficulties, triumphs, and areas for development. You can find patterns and gauge progression by keeping track of your progress.

Understanding Bouldering Routes and Problems

Every bouldering challenge offers a different puzzle to overcome. Understanding the grips, movements, and intended order is necessary when learning to read problems:

Maintain Identification:

Develop an initial plan by determining the hold kinds (crimps, jugs, slopers, etc.) and orientations.

Roadway Flow:

Examine the potential movement sequences and the orderly progression of grips. Determine which holds are essential for preserving balance and transitioning in advance.

Visualization:

Before tackling the course, mentally picture yourself ascending it. Your comprehension and performance can be improved by visualizing the sequence.

Working Through Cruxes and Sequences in Technical Issues

Every bouldering issue contains a crux, a difficult area that must be overcome using particular techniques:

Examining cruxes

By noticing where the difficulty increases, you can locate cruxes. Put your attention on comprehending the necessary body mechanics and skills.

Organizing Sequences:

The route should be divided into smaller portions, and each should be addressed separately. Create effective movement patterns for more seamless transitions.

Experimentation:

To solve cruxes, experiment with alternative methods. Finding the strategy that complements your strengths and learning style the best could require a few tries.

Techniques for Solving Issues and Beta

The secret to conquering obstacles and strengthening your bouldering abilities is to develop efficient problem-solving techniques:

Observation:

Check out how other climbers are approaching the similar challenge to get ideas for potential beta (movement patterns and approaches).

Collecting beta:

Engage in conversation with other climbers to exchange tips and strategies for certain problems. Sharing concepts can result in new insights.

Adapting Beta:

Adapt beta to your physical characteristics, skills, and weaknesses. For some climbers, what is optimal may not be for others.

Developing Strengths and Overcoming Stalls

Although plateaus are an inevitable aspect of growth, they can be overcame through hard work and determination:

Recognizing Weaknesses

Analyze your climbing performance to pinpoint your individual flaws. Focus on a single aspect, such as finger flexibility, strength, or technique.

Specific Training:

Spend time working on your deficiencies through targeted sessions, drills, and exercises. Introduce these areas gradually into your climbing program.

Diverse Training:

Use complementary workouts and cross-training to avoid burnout and keep a healthy level of fitness.

Physical and mental rest:

Overtraining or mental exhaustion may cause plateaus. Take breaks to rest and recover both physically and mentally.

Incremental Difficulties:

Increase the complexity of the issues you set for yourself gradually. Stasis is prevented by regular, small challenges.

In conclusion, progressing in bouldering is a complicated process that necessitates tenacity, flexibility, and problem-solving abilities. This trip requires a number of essential steps, including goal-setting, measuring progress, learning to read maps, overcoming obstacles, using problem-solving techniques, and training for weaknesses. Accept learning as a process, and see obstacles as chances to improve. In addition to its physical advantages, bouldering is a mental playground where creativity and tenacity are the keys to success. Keep in mind that each climber's journey is distinct, and that your dedication to growth will determine your experience and successes in the exciting world of bouldering.

CHAPTER SIX
BOULDERING OUTSIDE AND BEYOND

Entering the realm of outdoor bouldering brings up a world of unmatched obstacles, exquisite natural beauty, and a closer relationship with the environment. Outdoor bouldering offers a wide variety of terrains and experiences, while indoor bouldering offers a regulated environment. This guide examines the nuances of outdoor bouldering, including everything from selecting locations to moral issues, safety measures, overcoming obstacles, and embracing bouldering as a lifestyle.

Picking Bouldering Locations Outside

It's essential to choose the best outdoor bouldering locations for a secure and satisfying experience:

Research:

Utilize guidebooks, the internet, and the local climbing scene to conduct research on bouldering locations. Look for climbing sites that fit your tastes and skill level.

Accessibility and Rules:

Recognize any permit requirements, seasonal limits, and access restrictions for certain climbing places. Respect private property and follow any applicable local laws.

Ratings and grades:

Pay heed to bouldering areas' individual grading systems. From indoor climbing gyms, grades may vary and may have an impact on route choice.

Hardiness and Terrain:

Think about the local terrain and the level of severity of the issues. Sandstone, granite, or other types of rock with distinctive properties may be present in some places.

Morality and the Leave No Trace Guidelines

The obligation to protect the environment and keep good relations with the neighborhood community comes with outdoor bouldering:

Make No Trace:

Follow the Leave No Trace guidelines, which place a strong emphasis on reducing your environmental impact. Pack out all waste, don't harm the environment, and be mindful of the wildlife.

Observe any access limitations:

Observe any seasonal closures, closed areas, and other access limitations. Crossing lines can damage delicate ecosystems and cause access problems.

Little Impact:

Use brush grips sparingly, only when necessary, and prevent harming plants. To stop soil erosion, stick to well-established pathways.

Noise and disruption:

To avoid upsetting nearby wildlife and climbers, keep your volume respectfully low. Remember that some climbing places are close to homes.

Natural Environments and Bouldering Safety

Compared to indoor climbing, outdoor bouldering offers special safety considerations:

Zones for Scout Landing:

Check landing areas for any potential dangers like rocks, roots, or uneven ground. Clear the area of debris and utilize crash pads wisely.

Spotting:

Spotters can be used to direct your fall and make sure you land safely on crash pads. Clarify your communication with spotters to prevent confusion.

Communication:

With your climbing companions, establish clear communication. Before attempting a problem, talk about climbing plans, strategies, and safety precautions.

Emergency Planning:

Keep a first aid kit on you and be familiar with basic outdoor first aid.

Know how to treat typical climbing wounds like sprains or cuts.

Adapting to the Challenges of Outdoor Climbing

Outdoor climbing provides particular difficulties that necessitate flexibility and problem-solving abilities:

Climatic conditions

Be ready for the possibility of shifting weather. According to the prediction, pack layers of clothing, rain gear, sunscreen, and other necessities.

Typical Holds:

Compared to indoor holds, outdoor holds might be more challenging and unpredictable. Change the way you hold things and be careful around edges.

Route locating

Routes outside might not be as well signposted as issues inside. For precise route location, consult maps, reference books, and landmarks.

Environmental Change:

The altitude, humidity, and other environmental elements that can affect how well you climb outdoors differ. Adapt your strategy as necessary.

Bouldering as a Lifestyle: Connection and Exploration

Bouldering evolves from a purely physical pursuit to a way of life defined by camaraderie and exploration:

Establishing Contacts

Participate in regional gatherings, join climbing organizations, and network with other climbers to become involved in the outdoor bouldering scene. Creating connections improves the experience.

Visiting New Locations:

By climbing outside, you can discover breathtakingly beautiful natural settings. Each climbing location has a special combination of climbing difficulties and scenic beauty.

Mindful Investigation:
Take a meditative stance when climbing outside. Enjoy the surroundings, educate yourself

about the native flora and wildlife, and fully immerse yourself in the outdoors.

Personal Development

The mental and physical obstacles of outdoor bouldering promote personal development and self-discovery. Overcoming difficulties in nature increases fortitude and self-assurance.

In conclusion, bouldering outside offers a rich and varied experience that goes beyond the actual climbing. A holistic and fruitful experience is created by selecting appropriate bouldering locations, following to ethical principles, emphasizing safety, adjusting to outdoor challenges, and embracing bouldering as a lifestyle. Outdoor bouldering combines care for the environment, mindfulness, and a dedication to personal development to provide climbers with not only the chance to climb on actual rock but also the chance to connect with other climbers, discover stunning scenery, and develop a profound appreciation for the world around us.

THANK YOU

Printed in Great Britain
by Amazon